the raw healing of a numb heart

Holly Snow

The Raw Healing of a Numb Heart
by
Holly Snow
Copyright © Holly Snow 2018
Cover Copyright© Holly Snow 2018
Mountain High Publishing 2018

Thankyou to everyone who not only told me I could but believed it and encouraged me to believe it as well.

At a time when the pressure of life made me feel like I was suffocating, writing gave me air. This book is my heart and mind turned into words, and I'm putting it in your hands because it's time for the walls I've spent years building up to finally break down. Numb, Break, Grow, and Feel are the stages of life I've encountered in the process of making this book. I have never been so vulnerable to so many people, and I have never been more thankful to have been through the things I've experienced.

Over time I have learned that I am passionate about being the most stripped back version of whoever it is you are. Because no matter who you are...you are here, you are human, you are worthy, and you are loved. Life took me through some of my darkest moments only to show me that there is good on the other side of bad, and I needed to learn to love myself just as hard and just as deep as I loved others.

This book is proof that when I was living everyday in numbness and controlled by darkness, I still had enough strength to get through it. The people that have held on to me, regardless of how far I had fallen are the reason I am here. For everyone who has shown me life when I was so consumed by death, you are a part of this book. Here is the version of me behind the walls, this is our reminder that life is worth living. You are enough.

contents

Numb..6
Break..46
Grow...84
Feel..112

Numb

safe haven.

she guards her heart with a shield of titanium

protects her soul behind cement walls

this is the way she saves herself

even an honorable man will fall short to a love like hers

<u>fake it.</u>

smiles don't mean happy
and what a fool a person is to
believe they do

living on 'empty'.

i've gone through life claiming friends in all the wrong people.
but i don't want anymore empty relationships.
i want security in the ones i open my heart to.
i want honest love when i let my guard down.

trailer.

i let you get inside my head because on the surface you showed interest
but when you finally got a glimpse of who i was, you walked away like i was a movie you no longer wanted to see.

the reason i don't trust:1

he said he wanted to break my walls,
that he wanted to know me,
and he did.
he broke them, they crumbled,
and i stood there ripped apart
allowing it to happen.

risks.

at some point i'd like to feel
again
but i know the risk of letting you
in
giving you authority over my heart

so i hide behind my walls.
i will not fall and sadly,
this means i will not feel.

stained glass.

the glass barrier between you and me is my only protection.
the stained view behind it is the very depth of my being
tainted by the colors i choose to show you and your version of who i am
i will let you see me, but remember your place on the outside.

thoughts.

i'd love to be held captive in your mind.

<u>fine.</u>

saying "i'm fine" when you ask me
how i am is as honest as i can be.
fine is a place of in between.
between happiness and sadness,
that numb area.

i am not "hurting".
i am beaten down, but i do not
feel a thing.
i'm fine.

poison.

it was poison...
looking in the mirror, believing
that i wasn't enough
believing that i was wasted space,
that i was unworthy.
it was poison, but i kept drinking
it like i was dying of thirst.

speechless.

talking to you my bones stiffen, my heart shrivels, words burn the back of my throat.
i don't like talking about myself that means opening up, and i can't do that.

war.

you ruined me.

you saw that i was guarded and you begged for a way in.

so i rendered myself defenseless.

you made a grand entrance but you left in silence.

you caused chaos in my mind and made my heart into a battlefield.

you started war within me.

digging means dirt.

you dug into my soul

you saw it was dirty and damaged

so you took your shovel and left.

habit.

shivers down my spine
physical touch makes my body tense
swallowing the idea of a worthless
thing like me wasting your time
and space
i say "no."
my mind forms yet another layer of
bricks around my heart, blocking
you out
--then blocking myself out.

<u>work of art.</u>

my room is full of pictures and art
i've never liked bare walls
and maybe this is why there are so many drawings on my skin
my body is a canvas for my art
because i like to see the stories on the outside.

lies.

you fed me endless lies like they were the only thing worth believing, and i mistook them for sweet truth.

everything i don't have.

i am surrounded by hope
drenched in happiness
wrapped in love
but none of it is mine.

void.

i want all of this to mean something but my head is absent from my heart.
there are empty spaces in the places that used to overflow with emotion.
my soul has been thrown to the ground and kicked in
the dirt it's encountered has sunken deep within my roots, and suffocated every airway until all that's left is black...all that's left is void.

this is what i dream about.

if you ask me about my dreams i'll tell you i don't have any
but i've come to realize that my dream is happiness.
-to look in the mirror and be okay with what i see.
-to pull into the driveway at 1 a.m. and see you through the window sleeping because i had to work late.
-waking up to rushed mornings and messy schedules.
-coming home to my kids running wild when they should be in bed.
-to be hurt but aware and hopeful of the good that is to come.

my dream is to experience the reality of life and be happy with it.

depression.

depression is like a cement box that has no seal
you can not move, and every breath is harder than the last.
you can hear voices on the outside of all the people telling you to get out but no one that can help.
there is nothing that has loosened the cement, so here you are trying to adjust
but unless <u>you</u> are in this cement box <u>alone</u>, you are not aware of the weight that it is.

please do not tell someone with depression to just "get out."

emotional flatline.

an ice cold heart where even fire
could freeze
a body that matched the wreckage
of past lives
and bones that ached for healing
this life was draining
slowly slipping into demise
all feeling had escaped these
walls of skin called home.
paralyzed in an emotional
flatline.

independent.

she didn't let herself need anyone
she insisted on doing everything alone
because when she let people help
she let people in
and when she let people in she got hurt.

<u>benefits.</u>

scraping at my skin and digging at my bones just to feel something, leaving my body ruined but reminding me that i atleast had one.

and although my body had been desecrated and completely defaced -- you still wanted it because you liked the benefits.

<u>roses are red but i'm blue.</u>

you loved when i wore that red dress
always saying it was a good color on me
but i never felt good in that dress because in those moments i knew my body was the extent of what you saw and desired.
so as i stand here once again with my red dress on
--only to please you--
you can tell me that red looks good but
this type of red always makes me blue.

<u>broken.</u>

my heart was fractured

my mind was violated

my body was used

the scars on my skin were

intentionally placed

and emotions became another numb

space.

gasoline type of love.

loving you was like getting gasoline to fill my tank.
i was empty without it so i kept coming back for more, even if it was wasted on pointless destinations and outcomes.
i needed your love like gasoline because if i didn't have it, i couldn't move.

vandalized.

you spray painted black over my
bright heart to look like yours
beat me to the ground so we could
be level
but this is the type of love you
give
because it makes you feel good
and that kind of rush can get
addictive

unfixable.

when i was numb music was the only thing i could still feel
the only thing that reminded me i was human
but in those moments when i didn't feel human enough, i began
labeling myself as useless - like a broken record.
and as people walked in and out, giving up hope and treating me like i was unfixable,
life seemed like nothing more than white noise.
everything good was dull and the darkness was amplified.
so i laid there fighting for air as everybody left

i was the song nobody wanted to hear
and the music that no longer made me feel.

i will protect me.

i build walls around my heart
i deny love
i have numbed myself to every
feeling
isolated and barricaded,
allowing the only person capable
of destroying me to be myself.

so please do not try to unravel me
if you have no intention of
reaching my soul.

the reason i don't trust:2

for him to say something then
automatically move on as if he
never cared
has taught me that i am not worth
knowing
that there is no part of me that
is really, truly desired.
that real genuine love will never
be present because no matter how
much people say they care
there will always be something
that turns them away or makes them
think twice.

pieces.

please don't ask to have all of me...

i only know how to give in pieces.

anorexia.

"do you want dinner?"
--no thanks i had a late lunch
i didn't even eat lunch, or breakfast for that matter

"aren't you hungry? It's been 2 days."
--i haven't really had an appetite.
the past two days have been hell

"please eat your body is starting to shut down"
--no i'm okay, i feel fine.
i think i'm gonna pass out

"you need to eat, this many days without food will ruin your body"
--i've been good so far, and i'm not hungry.
it's been 5 days and i really have lost my appetite.

beneath my skin.

the thought of physical touch
makes me shake.
the act of physical touch
paralyzes me.
because physical things are
reasoned with emotions and those i
can not feel, express, or
understand.

so my body creates a fortress
within itself
just beneath my skin is a shield
allowing physical contact but
deflecting anything that goes
further
because these bones are weary and
dried, they can no longer rise
against
and under my skin,
deep within my soul and mind is a
dangerous place to be.

sweet relief.

the constant shadowy blueness of
my veins is concealed behind a
stream of red paint.
every couple seconds more paint is
made.
it runs down, falling into more of
itself
it stains over from the cracks in
my skin to where milky emulsion
overtakes the previously clear
water.

my adrenaline is present
but i can't kick it.
i like it.
for the first time in along time i
am suffocated by the sensation of
feeling.
i am aware of being alive.
i am relieved.

ecstasy.

being able to numb the numbness
was a high.

thank you Elton.

deafening music blasted through the stereo.
i played my music louder because it made everything more intense and
intensity causes people to feel something.
i used to listen to music as a way of coping with the pain
but the music has sealed itself into me when emotions did not.
now i listen to music to feel the heartbeat in my chest.

inhale-exhale love.

as you go around handing out
pieces of your heart on a silver
platter,
don't forget to feed yourself.
fill yourself with every ounce of
love you give.
allow yourself to receive what you
deserve.
let good things consume you, and
live in an ocean of
self-acceptance.

stop sinking in self-hate because
one day you'll be gasping for air
that air will be love
and nobody can provide that love
like you can.

<u>continue.</u>

i am human despite the fact that i can not feel...right now
because one day i will feel again.
i will understand my sadness in a different state, and i will meet happiness in a new light.
i am not done with this life.
i am numb right now, not forever.
i am going through some stuff.
this is what it means to be human.
and i will keep going.

Break

<u>i am nothing to you.</u>

you say you want my walls broken,
but when i tear them down it means
nothing to you.

deceit.

you looked like heaven
eyes that made someone feel at
home,
but you took them to hell instead.

we are all tired.

don't be mad when the clouds come out and the rain starts to fall. the storm is generous to take the spotlight once in a while sometimes the sun needs a break too.

you won the race.

you always liked going fast
ninety in a sixty
somewhere down the road you ran
into me but you didn't stop
you kept going and dragged my
heart on the ground behind you
like it was your trophy

obstacles.

vulnerability is my weakness.
isolation and self-destruction are
my strengths.

i know.

you used all my insecurities as your excuses to leave.
so yes, i know what it feels like to be so deep in that even the people you had the highest hopes for, have been searching for reasons to go.
yes, i know what it feels like to be giving your everything, yet constantly stuck in failure.
yes, i know what it's like to feel trapped in the pain.

you give me hell.

if i had a choice to cross a
bridge between heaven and hell,
i'd still choose hell
because being in heaven with you
is just the same.

sorry i wasn't enough.

my heart was scattered on the floor
each piece broken off for you and
you tossed these broken bits aside
like rubble in the way
because you were searching for
someone better

be there.

when the sun needs to sleep the
moon comes out to take her place
he watches over the earth when she
needs him to
he is ready for her when she is
too tired to go on.

<u>you're not indestructible.</u>

stop letting the pressure to do better kill your desire to live.

your mind is overwhelmed, so let it be

your body is tired, let it sleep.

less than dirt.

you were every beautiful thing a
person wanted
but that was just surface,
you were good at putting up a
front
denied any type of reality that
made you less desirable.

you let me think i was the one who
messed up
crumbled on the ground, sitting no
higher than dirt
because you were perfect,
and i was worthless.

<u>you make me nervous.</u>

someday i'd like to recognize the way your mouth curves when you kindly say my name
but all i know right now is the anger in your eyes when you see me,
and the shake of my voice when i speak.

words kill.

shooting hate at eachother like
bullets became our normal.
all we were trying to do was cause
pain as a way of justification
but each word was just a cover for
the pieces of our hearts we
refused to share...another excuse.
our conversations were based on
exhaustion and defeat.
the two of us were dead in our
hurt
fighting so hard to live so we
could give the pain to someone
else.

for you.

i'd turn myself inside out,
break myself into pieces
just to see you whole.

oppressed(holocaust).

confined and mistreated
overpowered by helplessness and isolation
you broke me down to my core
starved me of any chance of hope
so i laid on the ground weak and defeated
because in your eyes
i was not good enough.
not human enough to live and be loved.

tears.

salt water burns my cheeks and
stains my pillow,
but this is ritual - the only
thing constant in my life
salt water is mine, and he leaves
my body
in the same way people always
leave my heart
but somehow, salt water is always
there when i need him.

foolish.

constantly being around you was
like breathing in smoke,
toxic,
suffocating,
deadly,
but i stayed in hopes that the
next breath wouldn't kill me.

weighed down.

i let my constant questions about you eat me away.
why did i let you remove the armor i had so carefully placed around my heart?
why did i let you inside my head when i couldn't even do the same for myself?
i used harsh words like a sword to destroy any idea of intimacy and i put up defenses to shield out any act of love.
but now this armor is heavy,
this armor is crushing my heart.

a letter to my ex-best friend:

i'm finally at a loss,
all of my defenses have been
broken as i continue to sit here
in the discomfort of whatever we
are.
i have run out of anger, and as
usual i have pushed down all the
hurt.
a constant theme for me has been
becoming close with people that
come and go, unfortunately you
were one of them.
but as you leave, listen to every
"i'm sorry" that is yet to be
said.

i'm still stuck in the rhythm of
believing everything is my
fault...so i'm sorry that i let my
insecurities get in the way of
fixing things.

i'm sorry i never told you when i was hurt because i was too afraid of hurting you.
i'm sorry i didn't want to let you all the way in because "people always leave."
i'm sorry i never thanked you for saving me the way you deserve.
i'm sorry, i'll say it repeatedly until my tongue gets tired and my lungs are burning from lack of air.
and after all the "i'm sorry's", i will again be at a loss
because nothing will fix a one sided relationship between two people.

where we used to be.

we were the dangerous kids
young and reckless but at least my
heart was safe.
now we're not so much the same
at some point we grew up a little
protected our skin while our
hearts sunk to the back of our
chests
and shattered on the way down.

defeated.

i wake up everyday inside this same box of nothingness.
physical pain is not enough to keep me going, i want to feel something real.

1:18 a.m. - i am slipping.
my body is limp as i begin to fade
my lungs sink into desolation,
and my breath is no longer existent.
neither am i.

naked.

you tore away everything i covered myself with.
stripped me down until you reached my soul
and then you disappeared leaving me bare.

stop killing beauty.

when the snow falls it lays perfectly,
a soft layer of pure white and we drive over it turning it to dirty grey slush.
maybe we do this with life
we run over the beautiful things because we become more efficient when we create messes...
because it's easier to meet standards through a wrecked version of things.

bulimia.

you've become really good at rejecting things you've already accepted.

the meal you just ate starts to feel like a punch to the gut if you let it sit there too long and guilt is all you can think about until you are empty again.

maybe that's because you never allow yourself to be full of anything...

fully comfortable,

fully happy,

fully human.

you recognize "empty", and you can't really accept something if it's empty...if it's not there, but that's okay because you've become really good at rejecting things you've already accepted.

hara-kiri.

i suffocate myself in the
sensation of feeling and i know
i'm alive
but 'feeling alive' is the closest
i come to actually living and
sometimes i wish i could drive
that solace deeper.

the rubble in my life is heavy and
the desire to feel alive is
relentless.
this is self destruction.

the reason i don't trust:3

he had no intention of digging
deep
he just wanted the surface gone.
so to think about how i let
someone so close to me
only for them to break me and not
care about what was going on
inside,
left me drowning in my own mess.
this was the mess that i created.

undesired.

i'm sorry for being a weed when all you wanted was a flower.

i tend to be what everyone tries to avoid.

<u>if i go.</u>

i will walk around holding my head high, wearing a smile so the world will believe me when i tell them i'm okay.

but at night i think maybe it's better if i go
this is the moment where i let my head sink into my pillow because i get tired of holding it up.
this is the moment where i let the tears roll down my cheek because the smile was just a front, but i'm alone now.
this is the moment where i let insecurity seep through the wall i have built up
this is the moment where i let hell defeat me because in my mind, it would be easier for everyone else if i didn't exist.

<u>irrelevant at 11:55 p.m.</u>

the universe is consumed by unfathomably large galaxies containing stars that we think of as little
but this dim light we make wishes on is so massive that we are irrelevant to it.

living in the idea that we are all here for a purpose and thriving off the desire to impact the world,
we keep forgetting the smallness of our existence.
we lose the reality that we are on this planet to simply be.

dead body.

i know what it feels like for death to absorb itself into the pores of my skin.
when life is drained from the cracks in my lips and air has leaked out of my lungs only to consume my body replacing blood.
my heart has dragged itself to meet each beat and my brain chokes on itself trying to understand everything outside of my head.
my muscles have deteriorated under the pressure of my skin when death has seeped in.

sacrifice.

the tree drops his leaves so winter can be.
this is sacrifice.
this is beautiful.

yes, enough.

my stomach twists into itself as i sit on the bathroom floor, hair dangling down the side of the toilet bowl.
i return the meal i just ate in exchange for a better body, and on the rare occasion i don't return it,
i wear guilt like it is the prettiest dress in my closet.

is this enough?

the voice inside my head that says "you don't have to do this", that voice hides in the corners of my brain covered in shame overpowered by the voice shouting "you will never be enough."

so i wear my mask and put up a
guard in hopes that if people only
see the surface, they will
eventually want me.

is this enough?

i spend the day exhausting myself
believing that others will notice
and i pick myself back up because
there's no point in waiting around
for people who won't show.

is this enough?

the art i have painted on my body
is the result of pain,
these are the moments of weakness,
and absence of love.
everyday i force myself to be what
i don't let others be for me,

because i am scared i will not be good enough.

so please, tell me this is enough.

Grow

the old me.

weak

pathetic

unwanted

worthless

calling out every flaw

you made me feel small

inferior to everything

you made hell a place on earth and watched me burn.

little victory.

overtime i've learned that rolling with the punches doesn't mean not fighting back.
it means silently, and humbly winning.

confident light.

we look in the mirror and
criticize the shape of our bodies
claiming that we are "too big"
but we exist on a planet where the
sun and moon are not ashamed of
their size because beautiful
things are not afraid to be what
they are.

<u>find peace.</u>

close your eyes

quiet your mind

still your body, and let your soul

rest

the best is yet to come.

you and i were toxic
change became necessary
and walking away felt like
choosing death,
like i was asking to die
but in fact this was me beginning
to live.

realization.

all i can remember is how bad our relationship was
and how deeply i believed it was the only thing holding me together.

your version of endings.

the closure you were looking for
was never going to be found in
hurting me,
all you had to do was love
yourself.

worthy.

stop comparing yourself to
everything around you.
look at yourself with love not
hate,
because you deserve to be loved.

development.

flowers grow from the innermost
parts of your soul.
the surface of your being is
encapsulated in blossoms,
and beneath that is dirt.
but my dear, don't attempt to hide
the dirt in shame.
if you did not contain dirt,
you wouldn't grow flowers.

request.

please do not come back,
you will just ruin me again.

no more expectations.

i stopped expecting you.
no longer waiting for your name to
be the reason my phone lit up.
no longer caring whether or not
you noticed me.

once i realized that you were
unaffected by my existence,
i stopped being affected by yours.

whiskey over wine.

your words tasted like wine,
soft and sweet
but my dear i've always been more
of a whiskey girl.

we're all doing the same thing.
life is like driving
you have to slow down when you hit
a bump in the road
sometimes you have to stop, let
other people go first
and be aware of the people around
you,
recognize them but don't hesitate
when they leave.

it's not your fault.

learn to love you so no man ever has to,

learn to love you so that when they fail

you will not blame yourself.

claiming power.

the space between my legs is not
your home
you can't keep coming back and
claiming it to be yours once
everyone else has rejected you
the bed will be empty of my body
tonight
the place you return to every
night is worn out
between my legs is where you found
approval and believed it was love
so when the sun sets i won't be
there

good things.

petals bow at the sun's rising,
the one who makes them beautiful
has shown up day in and day out.

at the first drop of rain
the flowers will arch their backs,
they need to be fed in order to
live.

new friends.

i have known hate better than most things
rooted himself deep within me
i have known him to the core
and he has told me i am not worth living
he has lied to me endlessly

but i think it's time to meet love,
let me know her.

cleanse.

my life is dirty, my body is
scarred
so i will empty myself
i will pour out every ounce of my
being until complete vacancy.

release-refresh-renew,
all the dirt has been removed.

bold.

she was bold

she identified her fears

and simply said, "i don't care."

change is inevitable.

let change be the reason you open your mind,
but do not let it be the reason you close your heart.

choosing freedom.

i will free myself from insecurity and doubt
instead i will choose power
i am not a slave to myself
but the master of my own heart and
the ruler of my mind.

where light is necessary.

flowers do not bloom in darkness,

in darkness they are vulnerable

they wilt

they collapse

flowers require light to grow.

you call this love.

the soul crushing aggression in your violent screams immediately turned to sweet affection at your empty kisses
but i could still taste the absinthe that lingered on your lips
and finally i understood my value.

an untouchable woman.

be the kind of woman that stays
collected in moments of chaos
whose heart is made of gold and
whose mind is stronger than
diamonds
the kind of woman who knows her
worth
be the kind of woman who does not
give pieces of herself away in
search of "love" because
she has already loved herself
better than any man ever could

be the kind of man who respects a
woman like this.

change:

...something i ran away from for so long, but necessary for me to realize my worth.

Feel

known.

we exist on this planet to be
known by someone else
to exchange ideas, interests, and
emotions
random words and coexisting are
not our sole purpose
it is much deeper than that
if the very depths of our soul are
not known and connected to
another, this is wasted time.

safe.

i am not your safe

you can not place your secrets inside of me

you can not give me your prized possessions to hold

i will lock you out

i am not a safe

there is nothing valuable within me

i am not an object used to ensure someone else's security

i am not safe

i am wild and reckless

i destroy everything around me

opening up.

inside this book is every secret, every confession of who i am to the core of my existence this book has written everything down so when you read it please be careful...

this book is my heart.

life is a sunset.

i want to look at life as a sunset
to see each opportunity as a different color
to be mesmerized by the beauty of each breath i take
to be captured in the goodness of goodbye
to have hope for new beginnings and be still in faith that the sun will rise again tomorrow.

prayers.

i'd like to believe that somewhere on this earth i have a guardian angel
and i hope to God it's you.

voice.

the train of letters roll off my
tongue creating stories about
nothing
there is no point in the words
that are said,
but to be capable of speaking them
is an exhilarating thing
to feel the noise slide up the
back of my throat and reach
freedom,
listen to the collision of silence
and sound
the quiet is broken

this tongue is powerful
and these words put up a fight
this noise claims victory over the
silence
this voice is a weapon,
a sword that overcomes the battle.

<u>sick love.</u>

you were sick,
coughing up love for anybody like
it was killing you to save it for
someone special.

<u>anxiety.</u>

you know that moment where you
hold your breath for just a little
too long?
that's what anxiety feels like,
every breath feels like your lungs
are being filled until they're
about to pop but at the same time
you're not inhaling enough air
and when you let the air back out,
your chest feels like it shrivels
into itself deeper than each time
before

anxiety feels like drowning in
every thought you have, then
reaching a filter that allows you
but blocks out anything you could
possibly think
like you are water and your mind
is the fish

the net has separated and blocked
you from everything until you are
nothing

anxiety feels like your body is
shaking when its not
or maybe just the bones inside of
your skin trying to break loose
but it's impossible
trapped inside this wall that
holds all your pieces in place
you ache for a little bit of
freedom but skin stays
and maybe it's the only thing in
your life that has

anxiety is when your own body is
attacking you
the unfiltered thoughts sink down
into your chest and pile on your

lungs like rocks that crush any
hope of air

the air pushes out of your lungs
and fills your body leaving just
enough wiggle room for your bones
to rattle...in search of a way
that is never found

that is anxiety,
a control freak that has lost
control.

sleep in peace.

when the sun goes down and all
that's left is moon and stars
i want it to be you in the sheets
next to me,
my body in your arms.

she's everything.

she is warm like sunshine

cold like wind

she's a light breeze but stronger than thunder

unapologetically personal like rain

though she is an all consuming fire

drowning in freedom.

i submerge myself under the salty seas surface.
sinking deep,
i forget what it feels like to breathe in.
beneath the place where water and air kiss is where i embrace freedom.

weightless and unconfined.
celebrating the detachment of my flesh and toxic air.

i will not waste this moment.

<u>cold love.</u>

every moment with you felt like december.

your words were sharp icicles damaging my heart

you made me cold until i became numb

but even in your frozen bitterness,

i couldn't help myself from loving you.

to first period.

she was an angel with a little bit of devil
sweet but she had a temper
her beauty was undeniable
she had power in her confidence
with her heart set on the things she wanted,
she ran like hell after her dreams
and settled for nothing less than what she deserved
because she knew her worth and she was well aware of the fire inside her soul.

hug.

i feel our hearts beat in sync as
your arms hold my body still,
wrapped around my back like a
security blanket,
you are my safety net.

be love.

stop exhausting yourself by putting defenses between the love people give you and the hate you give yourself.

don't let your mind be a battle field for a war where the bad guy wins.

you've already earned love.

so *be* love

and love yourself,

you are worthy of it.

january 2014.

i burned incense because it smelled like smoke

my pop pops house smelled like smoke

on the bad days, incense smells like good memories.

a lonely reassurance.

we all feel desperate in the same moments...
when we're alone
when we need someone next to us in order to feel like the moment means something
...like we mean something.

adore you.

i crave to know you.

i want to know the feeling of your fingertips running down my back in slow motion.
i want to memorize the exact moments when your skin touches mine.
i want to feel our souls intertwining so deeply that i am physically shocked.
i want to see your mind in freedom.

i crave to know the intensity of your existence.

salty tears.

honey, you taste like salt water
and a different kind of life
let me weave myself into you,
i've always dreamed to be part of
the sea.

magic like this.

as we collapsed my head sunk into your chest
and all i could hear was heartbeat
the beat of someones heart so relaxed
perfectly paced

i never believed in magic until right now
and i would give anything to experience that moment forever.
i would trade everything to live in the magic that was your existence.

mourning.

mountains will collapse in the
earth's hands,
sunsets will turn black as night.
flowers will fold back into
themselves and droop over until
they are frowning at the ground.
water will be replaced by rock,
and a place we once freely jumped
will be deadly when you fall.

the universe will stop at the
sound of your soul crushing,
and everything will unfold again
when you rise to kiss moonlight.

<u>let love.</u>

you have to give yourself
permission to be loved
if you aren't allowing yourself to
be loved,
you aren't allowing yourself to
live.

i want you.

i will push through the wall that
is your chest,
the gates that are your ribs,
the life that fills your lungs,
the hell your heart is going
through
even if the bricks of your back
are crumbling
and too much good is seeping
through the cracks in your skin

leaving you unbalanced
bringing you to your knees and
chaining you down...
i will push through
because everything i want is found
in the moments spent with you.

<u>you.</u>

it's you,

you are the one that makes love feel like an ocean where i wouldn't mind drowning.

9:49 p.m.

i feel like my body is fading away,
like my skin isn't big enough to hold all the stuff inside
everything inside is expanding and pushing outward
but this flesh is not strong enough to hold it anymore

you are beautiful.

i believe that beauty is in *real* things,

things that make us human.

beauty is in flaws, passions, fears, and emotions.

and these my love, you do not lack.

galaxies.

your mind is made up of
extravagant galaxies
each thought as wild as fire
your eyes were planets...never
home, but i dreamed they would be.

you are a galaxy
but you only let me look from a
distance because there were stars
you never wanted me to see.

human.

she did not let just one emotion consume her
she wanted to feel everything at once
to be completely drenched in a sea of what it means to be human.

proof.

people always say "scars are proof
that you made it"
but i think the proof lies with
the heart in your chest that
hasn't stopped beating, and a mind
full of memories.

self-love.

do not let your heart bleed love for anyone more than it does for yourself.

the reason i can wear the shortsleeve shirt.

thankyou for loving me when there was nothing left to love.
you have been my strength in weakness and my laugh through tears.
you are the stars and moon tucked into skin.
dark and light wrapped themselves around you,
a sunbeam with glittery glow of moonlight.
i don't know how a marvel like you exists but you do
thankyou for seeing all of me even when i'm wearing the short sleeve shirt.

artist.

your fingertips have sculpted the very definition of love into life,
your palms have molded hearts into homes,
your hands have held charcoal and turned to touch beauty's face,
you have created masterpieces.

keep living.

i know that feeling...
the one where you can't find the point even though you've been searching in every direction.
the one where you are stuck right now and think you're gonna be there forever.

i know that feeling

the one where each breath feels like a punch to the chest because every second of life is a fight.
the one where your voice breaks and you know you're about to cry, but "maybe this time letting the tears out will make you feel better"... it never does.

i know that feeling

the one where life goes black and your mind goes empty - no more questions, no more random thoughts, no more connection.
and i think this one might be the hardest of all because even your own mind is fighting against you.

i know that feeling

the one where your body is rejecting you and you don't know how to keep going.
i get that, i lived that. i gave into that, and i tried to let that feeling win. but it didn't, and it won't.
i know your confusion, i gave up because i felt too weak to go on.

that feeling - the one you and i both know so well - it's real, but it is not you.

allow the feeling, you will break
yourself trying to fight it,
but allow the hope also because
you will kill yourself if you
don't have it.

stop strangling yourself.

i untangled vines to get to your heart
you are the type of person who suffocates yourself with everyone else because you think nobody could love you.
but beyond those vines is beauty in its purest form
let it untangle from you and breathe.

please continue;+

Made in the USA
Middletown, DE
06 August 2020